Rebekah !!

May your Journey
be safe + Peaceful
you will Always be in our
Our prayers. Now is the time
Stand and be strong in your
Faith in the Lord, And Also
a Responsible Adult, you will
Meet many new People And Experience
lot of different situations, but
I know our Lord will guide +
direct your PATH, with much
Love From us to you. Be
At Peace And be best
at what you do
Love Always
uncle H + I +
Darrell I +

To

Our sweet Niece Rebekah

From

uNcle Harold + Auntie Carolyn

THE *Joy* OF THE *Lord*
IS MY STRENGTH

A Treasury of
GOD'S PROMISES

summerside
PRESS

Summerside Press™
Minneapolis 55438
www.summersidepress.com

The Joy of the Lord Is My Strength
A Treasury of God's Promises
© 2010 Summerside Press™

ISBN 978-1-935416-55-5

Scripture references are from the following sources: The Holy Bible, King James Version (KJV). The Holy Bible, New International Version®, NIV®. Copyright © 1973, 1978, 1984 by International Bible Society. Used by permission of Zondervan. The New King James Version (NKJV). Copyright © 1982 by Thomas Nelson, Inc. Used by permission. The Holy Bible, English Standard Version® (ESV), copyright © 2001 by Crossway Bibles, a publishing ministry of Good News Publishers. Used by permission. The New American Standard Bible® (NASB), Copyright © 1960, 1962, 1963, 1968, 1971, 1972, 1973, 1975, 1977, 1995 by The Lockman Foundation. Used by permission. The Holy Bible, New Living Translation (NLT), copyright 1996, 2004. Used by permission of Tyndale House Publishers, Inc., Wheaton, Illinois. *The Message*. Copyright © 1993, 1994, 1995, 1996, 2000, 2001, 2002 by Eugene Peterson. Used by permission of NavPress, Colorado Springs, CO.

Compiled by Marilyn Jansen
Designed by Jenny Bethke
Cover image by istockphoto.com

Summerside Press™ is an inspirational publisher offering fresh, irresistible books to uplift the heart and engage the mind.

Printed in China

CONTENTS

MY STRONGHOLD

The LORD made the heavens.
Splendor and majesty are before him;
strength and joy in his dwelling place.

1 CHRONICLES 16:26-27 NIV

The LORD is the strength of his people,
a fortress of salvation for his anointed one.

PSALM 28:8 NIV

Be exalted, O LORD, in Your strength;
We will sing and praise Your power.

PSALM 21:13 NASB

The joy of the LORD is your strength.

NEHEMIAH 8:10 KJV

I shall joyfully sing
of Your lovingkindness in the morning,
For You have been my stronghold
And a refuge in the day of my distress.
O my strength, I will sing praises to You;
For God is my stronghold,
the God who shows me lovingkindness.

PSALM 59:16-17 NASB

The joy of Jesus will be my strength—
it will be in my heart. Every person
I meet will see it in my work,
my walk, my prayer—in everything.

— *Mother Teresa* —

KNOW THE LORD

"Behold, God is my salvation,
I will trust and not be afraid;
For the LORD GOD is my strength and song,
And He has become my salvation."
Therefore you will joyously draw water
from the springs of salvation.

ISAIAH 12:2-3 NASB

Do not cast me away from Your presence
And do not take Your Holy Spirit from me.
Restore to me the joy of Your salvation
And sustain me with a willing spirit.
Then I will teach transgressors Your ways,
And sinners will be converted to You.

PSALM 51:11-13 NASB

There will be heard once more the sounds
of joy and gladness...saying,
"Give thanks to the Lord Almighty,
for the Lord is good; his love endures forever."

JEREMIAH 33:10-11 NIV

*As we enter more and more
deeply into this experience...our knowledge
of God increases, and with it our peace,
our strength and our joy. God help us,
then...that we all may in truth
"know the Lord."*

— *J. I. Packer* —

HARMONIOUS SONG

I will bless the LORD at all times:
his praise shall continually be in my mouth.

PSALM 34:1 KJV

Let the heavens rejoice, let the earth be glad;
let them say among the nations,
"The LORD reigns!"
Let the sea resound, and all that is in it;
let the fields be jubilant, and everything in them!
Then the trees of the forest will sing,
they will sing for joy before the LORD,
for he comes to judge the earth.
Give thanks to the LORD, for he is good;
his love endures forever.

1 CHRONICLES 16:31–34 NIV

You'll go out in joy, you'll be led into a whole
and complete life. The mountains and hills will
lead the parade, bursting with song.
All the trees of the forest will join
the procession, exuberant with applause.

ISAIAH 55:12 THE MESSAGE

True Christian joy is the heart's
harmonious response to the
Lord's song of love.

— *A. W. Tozer* —

PEACE IN GOD

Let the light of your face shine upon us, O Lord.
You have filled my heart with greater joy
than when their grain and new wine abound.
I will lie down and sleep in peace,
for you alone, O Lord,
make me dwell in safety.

PSALM 4:6-8 NIV

Now the God of hope fill you
with all joy and peace in believing.

ROMANS 15:13 KJV

When I said, "My foot is slipping,"
your love, O Lord, supported me.
When anxiety was great within me,
your consolation brought joy to my soul.

PSALM 94:18-19 NIV

Deceit is in the heart of those who devise evil,
but those who plan peace have joy.

PROVERBS 12:20 ESV

The kingdom of God is not eating and drinking,
but righteousness and peace and joy in the Holy
Spirit. For he who in this way serves Christ is
acceptable to God and approved by men.

ROMANS 14:17-18 NASB

*Joy is not happiness so much
as gladness; it is the ecstasy of eternity
in a soul that has made peace with God
and is ready to do His will.*

15

INTEGRITY OF HEART

I will sing of steadfast love and justice;
to you, O LORD, I will make music.
I will ponder the way that is blameless....
I will walk with integrity of heart
within my house.

PSALM 101:1-2 ESV

I know, my God, that you test the heart and are
pleased with integrity. All these things have I
given willingly and with honest intent. And now
I have seen with joy how willingly your people
who are here have given to you. O LORD,
God of our fathers Abraham, Isaac and Israel,
keep this desire in the hearts of your people
forever, and keep their hearts loyal to you.

1 CHRONICLES 29:17-18 NIV

In everything set them an example by doing
what is good. In your teaching show integrity,
seriousness and soundness of speech that cannot
be condemned, so that those who oppose you
may be ashamed because they have nothing
bad to say about us.

TITUS 2:7-8 NIV

The beauty of a house is harmony.
The security of a house is loyalty.
The joy of a house is love.

— *Frank Crane* —

SHOUT FOR JOY

Shout for joy to God, all the earth;

sing the glory of his name;

give to him glorious praise!

Say to God, "How awesome are your deeds!"

PSALM 66:1-3 ESV

Let all those rejoice who put their trust in You;

Let them ever shout for joy, because You defend them;

Let those also who love Your name Be joyful in You.

For You, O LORD, will bless the righteous;

With favor You will surround him as with a shield.

PSALM 5:11-12 NKJV

He will yet fill your mouth with laughter and

your lips with shouts of joy.

JOB 8:21 NIV

May we shout for joy over your salvation,
and in the name of our God set up our banners!
May the LORD fulfill all your petitions!

PSALM 20:5 ESV

Be glad in the LORD, and rejoice, O righteous,
and shout for joy, all you upright in heart!

PSALM 32:11 ESV

*Through all eternity to Thee
A joyful song I'll raise;
For oh! eternity's too short
To utter all Thy praise.*

— Joseph Addison —

CIRCUMSTANCES

And now my head shall be lifted up
above my enemies all around me,
and I will offer in his tent
sacrifices with shouts of joy;
I will sing and make melody to the LORD.

PSALM 27:6 ESV

Rejoice in the Lord always; again I will say,
rejoice!... Be anxious for nothing, but in
everything by prayer and supplication with
thanksgiving let your requests be made known
to God. And the peace of God, which surpasses
all comprehension, will guard your hearts and
your minds in Christ Jesus.

PHILIPPIANS 4:4, 6-7 NASB

For you make him most blessed forever;
you make him glad with the joy of your presence.
For the king trusts in the LORD,
and through the steadfast love of the Most High
he shall not be moved.

PSALM 21:6-7 ESV

*The miracle of joy is this:
It happens when there is no apparent
reason for it. Circumstances may call
for despair. Yet something different rouses
itself inside us.... We remember God.*

— Ruth Senter —

PERSEVERANCE

Blessed is the man who perseveres under trial, because when he has stood the test, he will receive the crown of life that God has promised to those who love him.

JAMES 1:12 NIV

As you know, we consider blessed those who have persevered. You have heard of Job's perseverance and have seen what the Lord finally brought about. The Lord is full of compassion and mercy.

JAMES 5:11 NIV

And let us not grow weary while doing good, for in due season we shall reap if we do not lose heart.

GALATIANS 6:9 NKJV

Let us fix our eyes on Jesus, the author and perfecter of our faith, who for the joy set before him endured the cross, scorning its shame, and sat down at the right hand of the throne of God.

HEBREWS 12:2 NIV

*How could we know the joy
without the suffering?
And how could we endure the suffering
but that we are warmed and carried
on the breast of God?*

— *Desmond M. Tutu* —

SING FOR JOY

Surely you have granted him eternal blessings
and made him glad with the joy of your presence.

PSALM 21:6 NIV

I will praise You with the harp
for your faithfulness, O my God;
I will sing praise to you with the lyre,
O Holy One of Israel.
My lips will shout for joy
when I sing praise to you—
I, whom you have redeemed.

PSALM 71:22-23 NIV

O sing unto the LORD a new song:
sing unto the LORD, all the earth.

PSALM 96:1 KJV

Satisfy us in the morning with your unfailing love,
that we may sing for joy and be glad all our days.

*Our hearts were made for joy. Our hearts
were made to enjoy the One who created them.
Too deeply planted to be much affected by
the ups and downs of life, this joy
is a knowing and a being known
by our Creator. He sets our hearts alight
with radiant joy.*

CREATION
REJOICES

The little hills rejoice on every side.
The pastures are clothed with flocks;
The valleys also are covered with grain;
They shout for joy, they also sing.

PSALM 65:12-13 NKJV

Let the sea roar, and all its fullness,
the world and those who dwell in it;
Let the rivers clap their hands;
Let the hills be joyful together
before the LORD.

PSALM 98:7-9 NKJV

Praise the LORD from the earth,
you great sea creatures and all ocean depths,
lightning and hail, snow and clouds.

PSALM 148:7-8 NIV

Let the heavens rejoice, let the earth be glad;

let the sea resound, and all that is in it;

let the fields be jubilant, and everything in them.

Then all the trees of the forest will sing for joy.

PSALM 96:11-13 NIV

I look up and try to understand that our solar system is a tiny pinprick in that great river of stars…. The truth I hold to is that it is all God's, joyfully created, and that it is good.

— *Madeleine L'Engle* —

THE JOY OF FRIENDS

A friend loves at all times,
and a brother is born for adversity.

PROVERBS 17:17 NKJV

Two are better than one,
Because they have a good reward for their labor.
For if they fall, one will lift up his companion.
But woe to him who is alone when he falls,
For he has no one to help him up.

ECCLESIASTES 4:9-10 NKJV

We have great joy and consolation
in your love, because the hearts of the saints
have been refreshed by you.

PHILEMON 1:7 NKJV

I rejoice greatly in the Lord that at last
you have renewed your concern for me.
Indeed, you have been concerned,
but you had no opportunity to show it.

PHILIPPIANS 4:10 NIV

A real friend sticks closer than a brother.

PROVERBS 18:24 NLT

*A friend is a solace in grief
and in joy a merry companion.*

— *John Lyly* —

ABUNDANT BLESSINGS

He split rocks in the wilderness
and gave them drink abundantly as from the deep.
He made streams come out of the rock
and caused waters to flow down like rivers.

PSALM 78:15-16 ESV

How blessed is the man who fears the LORD,
Who greatly delights in His commandments.
His descendants will be mighty on earth;
The generation of the upright will be blessed.
Wealth and riches are in his house,
And his righteousness endures forever.
Light arises in the darkness for the upright;
He is gracious and compassionate and righteous.

PSALM 112:1-5 NASB

Now to him who is able to do far more
abundantly than all that we ask or think,
according to the power at work within us,
to him be glory in the church and in Christ Jesus
throughout all generations, forever and ever.

EPHESIANS 3: 20-21 ESV

However many blessings we expect
from God, His infinite liberality
will always exceed all our
wishes and our thoughts.

— John Calvin —

PURPOSE AND JOY

The plans of the LORD stand firm forever,
the purposes of his heart through all generations.
Blessed is the nation whose God is the LORD,
the people he chose for his inheritance.

PSALM 33:11-12 NIV

Make my joy complete by being
of the same mind, maintaining the same love,
united in spirit, intent on one purpose.

PHILIPPIANS 2:2 NASB

The LORD will fulfill his purpose for me;
your love, O LORD, endures forever —
do not abandon the works of your hands.

PSALM 138:8 NIV

May He grant you according to your heart's desire,
And fulfill all your purpose.
We will rejoice in your salvation,
And in the name of our God
we will set up our banners!
May the LORD fulfill all your petitions.

PSALM 20:4–5 NKJV

*Joy is the holy fire that keeps our
purpose warm and our intelligence aglow.*

— *Helen Keller* —

DELIGHT
IN HIS WORD

Your testimonies are my heritage forever,
for they are the joy of my heart.
I incline my heart to perform your statutes
forever, to the end.

PSALM 119:111-112 ESV

Make me walk in the path of Your commandments,
For I delight in it.

PSALM 119:35 NASB

I have rejoiced in the way of Your testimonies,
As much as in all riches.
I will meditate on Your precepts
And regard Your ways.
I shall delight in Your statutes;
I shall not forget Your word.

PSALM 119:14-16 NASB

I find my delight in your commandments,
which I love.
I will lift up my hands toward your
commandments, which I love,
and I will meditate on your statutes.

PSALM 119:47-48 ESV

Great are the works of the LORD;
they are pondered by all who delight in them.

PSALM 111:2 NIV

*God cannot give us a happiness and
peace apart from Himself, because it is
not there. There is no such thing.*

— *C.S. Lewis* —

CREATOR OF JOY

The heavens are telling of the glory of God;
And their expanse is declaring
the work of His hands.
Day to day pours forth speech,
And night to night reveals knowledge.

PSALM 19:1-2 NASB

Be glad and rejoice forever in what I create;
For behold, I create Jerusalem for rejoicing
And her people for gladness.

ISAIAH 65:18 NASB

Ask and you will receive,
and your joy will be complete.

JOHN 16:24 NIV

You have turned for me my mourning into dancing;
You...have girded me with gladness,
That my soul may sing praise to You
and not be silent
O LORD my God, I will give thanks
to You forever.

PSALM 30:11-12 NASB

*To the children of God there stands,
behind all that changes and can change,
only one unchangeable joy. That is God.*

— Hannah Whitall Smith —

SATISFIED IN HIM

How lovely are Your dwelling places,
O LORD of hosts!
My soul longed and even yearned
for the courts of the LORD;
My heart and my flesh sing for joy to the living God....
For a day in Your courts is better than a
thousand outside.

PSALM 84:1-2, 10 NASB

Though you have not seen him, you love him;
and even though you do not see him now,
you believe in him and are filled with an
inexpressible and glorious joy.

1 PETER 1:8 NIV

It is a good thing to receive wealth from God
and the good health to enjoy it. To enjoy your
work and accept your lot in life—this is indeed
a gift from God. God keeps such people...
busy enjoying life.

ECCLESIASTES 5:19-20 NLT

All my springs of joy are in you.

PSALM 87:7 NASB

*God is most glorified in us
when we are most satisfied in Him.*

— *John Piper* —

JOY IN THE MORNING

Those living far away fear your wonders;
where morning dawns and evening fades
call forth songs of joy.

PSALM 65:8 NIV

For his anger is but for a moment,
and his favor is for a lifetime.
Weeping may tarry for the night,
but joy comes with the morning.

PSALM 30:5 ESV

Let me hear in the morning of your steadfast love,
for in you I trust.
Make me know the way I should go,
for to you I lift up my soul.

PSALM 143:8 ESV

O LORD, be gracious to us;

we long for you.

Be our strength every morning,

our salvation in time of distress.

ISAIAH 33:2 NIV

Hold on, my child!

Joy comes in the morning!

The darkest hour means

dawn is just in sight!

— *Gloria Gaither* —

BLESSING
OF FAMILY

Children's children are the crown of old men,

And the glory of children is their father.

PROVERBS 17: 6 NKJV

Behold, children are a gift of the LORD,

The fruit of the womb is a reward.

Like arrows in the hand of a warrior,

So are the children of ones youth.

How blessed is the man whose quiver is full of them;

They will not be ashamed

When they speak with their enemies in the gate.

PSALM 127:3-5 NASB

He gives the barren woman a home, making her

the joyous mother of children. Praise the Lord!

PSALM 113:9 ESV

Jesus called for them, saying, "Permit the children to come to Me, and do not hinder them, for the kingdom of God belongs to such as these."

LUKE 18:16 NASB

I have no greater joy than this, to hear of my children walking in the truth.

3 JOHN 1:4 NASB

Perhaps the greatest social service that can be rendered by anybody to the country and to mankind is to bring up a family.

— *George Bernard Shaw* —

OUR PROVIDER

Sing to the LORD with thanksgiving...
Who covers the heavens with clouds,
Who provides rain for the earth,
Who makes grass to grow on the mountains.

PSALM 147:7-8 NASB

And God will generously provide all you need.
Then you will always have everything you need
and plenty left over to share with others.

2 CORINTHIANS 9:8 NLT

What a help you are to the weak!
How you have saved the arm without strength!
What counsel you have given to one without wisdom!
What helpful insight you have abundantly provided!

JOB 26:2-3 NASB

The eyes of all look to you,
and you give them their food in due season.
You open your hand;
you satisfy the desire of every living thing.
The LORD is righteous in all his ways
and kind in all his works.

PSALM 145:15-17 ESV

*Thank God that even when we are not
worthy of His blessings, He still loves
us and bestows peace, joy, and happiness.*

— Gary Smalley and John Trent —

JOY IN HIS HOUSE

I would rather be a gatekeeper in the house of my God
than live the good life in the homes of the wicked.
For the LORD God is our sun and our shield.
He gives us grace and glory.
The LORD will withhold no good thing from
those who do what is right.

PSALM 84:10-11 NLT

The children of men…are abundantly satisfied
with the fullness of Your house,
and You give them drink from
the river of Your pleasures.
For with You is the fountain of life;
In Your light we see light.

PSALM 36:7-9 NKJV

By Your abundant lovingkindness
I will enter Your house,
At Your holy temple I will bow
in reverence for You.
O LORD, lead me in Your righteousness because
of my foes;
Make Your way straight before me.

PSALM 5:7-8 NASB

*I would not give one moment of heaven
for all the joys and riches of the world,
even if it lasted for thousands and
thousands of years.*

— *Martin Luther* —

BOUNTIFUL BLESSINGS

The LORD will command the blessing on you
in your storehouses and in all to which you set
your hand, and He will bless you in the land
which the LORD your God is giving you.
The LORD will establish you as a holy people to
Himself, just as He has sworn to you,
if you keep the commandments of the LORD
your God and walk in His ways.

DEUTERONOMY 28:8-9 NKJV

The humble will inherit the land
And will delight themselves
in abundant prosperity.

PSALM 37:11 NASB

From the fullness of his grace we have all
received one blessing after another.
For the law was given through Moses;
grace and truth came through Jesus Christ.

JOHN 1:16-17 NIV

When seeds of kindness are sown
prayerfully in the garden plot of
our lives, we may be sure that there
will be a bountiful harvest of blessings
for both us and others.

— *W. Phillip Keller* —

PATHS OF LIFE

You have made known to me the paths of life;

you will fill me with joy in your presence.

ACTS 2:28 NIV

Send forth your light and your truth,

let them guide me;

let them bring me to your holy mountain,

to the place where you dwell.

Then will I go to the altar of God,

to God, my joy and my delight.

PSALM 43:3-4 NIV

You make known to me the path of life;

in your presence there is fullness of joy;

at your right hand are pleasures forevermore.

PSALM 16:11 ESV

Trust in the LORD with all your heart,
And lean not on your own understanding;
In all your ways acknowledge Him,
And He shall direct your paths.

PROVERBS 3:5-6 NKJV

Not merely does God will to guide us by showing us His way...whatever mistakes we may make, we shall come safely home. Slippings and strayings there will be, no doubt, but the everlasting arms are beneath us.

— J. I. Packer —

A SECURE FUTURE

Surely goodness and love will follow me
all the days of my life,
and I will dwell in the house of the Lord
forever.

PSALM 23:6 NIV

"For I know the plans that I have for you,"
declares the Lord, "plans for welfare and not
for calamity to give you a future and a hope."

JEREMIAH 29:11 NASB

O Lord, you are my God;
I will exalt you; I will praise your name,
for you have done wonderful things,
plans formed of old, faithful and sure.

ISAIAH 25:1 ESV

In the future there is laid up for me the
crown of righteousness, which the Lord,
the righteous Judge, will award to me on
that day; and not only to me, but also
to all who have loved His appearing.

2 TIMOTHY 4:8 NASB

*Has this world been so kind to you
that you should leave with regret?
There are better things ahead than
any we leave behind.*

— C.S. Lewis —

HE IS GOOD

Now therefore arise, O LORD God,
to Your resting place, You and the ark
of Your might; let Your priests, O LORD God,
be clothed with salvation and let
Your godly ones rejoice in what is good.

2 CHRONICLES 6:41 NASB

The steps of a good man are ordered by the LORD,
And He delights in his way.

PSALM 37:23 NKJV

I will praise you forever for what you have done;
in your name I will hope, for your name is good.
I will praise you in the presence of your saints.

PSALM 52:9 NIV

I believe that I shall look upon
the goodness of the LORD
in the land of the living!

PSALM 27:13 ESV

*Even when all we see are the tangled
threads on the backside of life's tapestry,
we know that God is good and is out
to do us good always.*

— *Richard J. Foster* —

DELIVERANCE

You are my hiding place;
You preserve me from trouble;
You surround me with songs of deliverance.

PSALM 32:7 NASB

My heart rejoices in the LORD; in the LORD
my horn is lifted high. My mouth boasts over
my enemies, for I delight in your deliverance.

1 SAMUEL 2:1 NIV

The LORD is my rock and my fortress and
my deliverer, my God, my rock, in whom I take
refuge, my shield, and the horn of my salvation,
my stronghold and my refuge, my savior.

2 SAMUEL 22:2-3 ESV

Let us then with confidence draw near to the throne of grace, that we may receive mercy and find grace to help in time of need.

HEBREWS 4:16 ESV

I look for your deliverance, O LORD.

GENESIS 49:18 NIV

The beauty of grace—our only permanent
deliverance from guilt—is that
it meets us where we are
and gives us what we don't deserve.

— *Charles R. Swindoll* —

JOY AND HARMONY

It is good to give thanks to the LORD,

to sing praises to your name, O Most High;

to declare your steadfast love in the morning,

and your faithfulness by night,

to the music of the lute and the harp,

to the melody of the lyre.

For you, O LORD, have made me

glad by your work;

at the works of your hands I sing for joy.

PSALM 92:1-4 ESV

Shout joyfully to the LORD, all the earth.

Serve the LORD with gladness;

Come before Him with joyful singing.

PSALM 100:1-2 NASB

Make a joyful noise to the LORD,
all the earth;
break forth into joyous song
and sing praises!
Sing praises to the LORD with the lyre,
with the lyre and the sound of melody!

PSALM 94:4-5 ESV

*It is right and good that we...
give thanks and praise to You, O God.
We worship You, we confess to You,
we praise You, we bless You, we sing
to You, and we give thanks to You.*

— *Lancelot Andrews* —

TRUST THE LORD

I have set the LORD continually before me;
Because He is at my right hand, I will not be shaken.
Therefore my heart is glad and my glory rejoices;
My flesh also will dwell securely.

PSALM 16:8-9 NASB

In returning and rest you shall be saved;
in quietness and in trust shall be your strength.

ISAIAH 30:15 ESV

For He will give His angels charge concerning you,
To guard you in all your ways.
They will bear you up in their hands,
That you do not strike your foot against a stone.

PSALM 91:11-12 NASB

How blessed is everyone who fears the LORD,

Who walks in His ways.

When you shall eat of the fruit of your hands,

You will be happy and it will be well with you.

PSALM 128:1-2 NASB

My prayer is that I would learn to trust You more. It's such a comfort to know that my life is in Your hands.... May I find my strength in Your joy.

— Kim Boyce —

THROUGH
TROUBLE

On the day I called, You answered me;
You made me bold with strength in my soul….
For great is the glory of the LORD.
For though the LORD is exalted,
Yet He regards the lowly….
Though I walk in the midst of trouble,
You will revive me;
You will stretch forth Your hand…
and Your right hand will save me.

PSALM 138:3, 5-7 NASB

Peace I leave with you, My peace I give to you;
not as the world gives do I give to you. Let not
your heart be troubled, neither let it be afraid.

JOHN 14:27 NKJV

The LORD is good, a refuge in times of trouble.
He cares for those who trust in him.

NAHUM 1:7 NIV

Who shall separate us from the love of Christ?
Shall trouble or hardship or persecution?...
No, in all these things we are more than
conquerors through him who loved us.

ROMANS 8:35, 37 NIV

Life need not be easy to be joyful.
Joy is not the absence of trouble,
but the presence of Christ.

— *William Vanderhoven* —

JOY OF HEAVEN

They will enter Zion with singing;
everlasting joy will crown their heads.
Gladness and joy will overtake them,
and sorrow and sighing will flee away.

ISAIAH 35:10 NIV

Rejoice in hope, be patient in tribulation,
be constant in prayer.

ROMANS 12:12 ESV

Why are you downcast, O my soul?
Why so disturbed within me?
Put your hope in God,
for I will yet praise him,
my Savior and my God.

PSALM 42:5-6 NIV

In the shadow of Your wings I sing for joy.

PSALM 63:7 NASB

He has shown kindness by giving you rain
from heaven and crops in their seasons;
he provides you with plenty of food
and fills your hearts with joy.

ACTS 14:17 NIV

*No one need be downcast, for Jesus is
the joy of heaven, and it is His joy
to enter into sorrowful hearts.*

— *Frederick W. Faber* —

OVERCOMING

In the world you will have tribulation; but be
of good cheer, I have overcome the world.

JOHN 16:33 NKJV

I lie down and sleep;
I wake again, because the LORD sustains me.
I will not fear the tens of thousands
drawn up against me on every side.

PSALM 3:5-6 NIV

Do not be afraid of them. Remember the Lord,
who is great and awesome, and fight for your
brothers, your sons, your daughters, your wives,
and your homes.... Our God will fight for us.

NEHEMIAH 4:14, 20 ESV

Everyone born of God overcomes the world.
This is the victory that has overcome the world,
even our faith…. Who is it that overcomes
the world? Only he who believes that
Jesus is the Son of God.

1 JOHN 5:4–5 NIV

*The things we try to avoid and fight
against—tribulation, suffering, and
persecution—are the very things that
produce abundant joy in us.*

— *Oswald Chambers* —

LOVE GOD

Love GOD, your God. Walk in his ways.
Keep his commandments, regulations, and rules
so that you will live, really live, live exuberantly,
blessed by GOD…. Love GOD, your God,
listening obediently to him,
firmly embracing him. Oh yes, he is life itself.

DEUTERONOMY 30:16, 20 THE MESSAGE

My steadfast love I will keep for him forever,
and my covenant will stand firm for him.

PSALM 89:28 ESV

You shall love the LORD your God
with all your heart, with all your soul,
and with all your strength.

DEUTERONOMY 6:5 NKJV

I have hidden your word in my heart
that I might not sin against you.
Praise be to you, O LORD;
teach me your decrees.

PSALM 119:11-12 NIV

Only God can truly comfort;
There is the whisper of His love,
the joy of His presence, and the shining
of His face, for those who love Jesus
for Himself alone.

— Susan B. Strachan —

JOYFUL PLAY

I will be glad and exult in you;
I will sing praise to your name, O Most High.

PSALM 9:2 ESV

I commend the enjoyment of life, because
nothing is better for a man under the sun than
to eat and drink and be glad. Then joy will
accompany him in his work all the days of
the life God has given him under the sun.

ECCLESIASTES 8:15 NIV

Sing to him a new song;
play skillfully, and shout for joy.

PSALM 33:3 NIV

And so, my children, listen to me;
for all who follow my ways are joyful.

PROVERBS 8:32 NLT

*The real joy of life is in its play....
It is the real living of life with the
feeling of freedom and self-expression.
Play is the business of childhood,
and its continuation in later years is
the prolongation of youth.*

— Walter Rauschenbusch —

MY HELPER

The LORD is my strength and my shield;
my heart trusts in him, and I am helped.
My heart leaps for joy
and I will give thanks to him in song.

PSALM 28:7 NIV

I lift up my eyes to the hills—
where does my help come from?
My help comes from the LORD,
the Maker of heaven and earth.
He will not let your foot slip—
he who watches over you will not slumber;
indeed, he who watches over Israel
will neither slumber nor sleep.

PSALM 121:1-4 NIV

Trust the LORD!

He is your helper and your shield.

All you who fear the LORD, trust the LORD!

He is your helper and your shield.

PSALM 115:10-11 NLT

We have a Father in heaven...who loves His children as He loves His only-begotten Son, and whose very joy and delight it is to succor and help them at all times and under all circumstances.

— *George Müller* —

CONTENTMENT

Now there is great gain in godliness
with contentment, for we brought nothing
into the world, and we cannot take anything out
of the world. But if we have food and clothing,
with these we will be content.

1 TIMOTHY 6:6-8 ESV

I have learned to be content in whatever
circumstances I am. I know how to get along
with humble means, and I also know how to live
in prosperity; in any and every circumstance
I have learned the secret of being filled
and going hungry, both of having abundance
and suffering need.

PHILIPPIANS 4:11-12 NASB

For he will not dwell unduly on the days
of his life, because God keeps him busy
with the joy of his heart.

ECCLESIASTES 5:20 NKJV

*Finding acceptance with joy, whatever
the circumstances of life—whether they are
petty annoyances or fiery trials—
this is a living faith that grows.*

— *Mary Lou Steigleder* —

Make my joy complete by being like-minded,
having the same love, being one in spirit
and purpose. Do nothing out of selfish ambition
or vain conceit, but in humility consider others
better than yourselves.

PHILIPPIANS 2:2-3 NIV

Have unity of mind, sympathy, brotherly love,
a tender heart, and a humble mind. Do not
repay evil for evil or reviling for reviling, but on
the contrary, bless, for to this you were called,
that you may obtain a blessing.

1 PETER 3:8-9 ESV

In everything, do to others
what you would have them do to you.

MATTHEW 7:12 NIV

Be kindly affectionate to one another
with brotherly love, in honor giving
preference to one another.

ROMANS 12:10 NKJV

This I command you, that you love one another.

JOHN 15:17 NASB

*The joy that you give to others
is the joy that comes back to you.*

— *John Greenleaf Whittier* —

GRACE
FOR TRIALS

Count it all joy when you fall into various trials,
knowing that the testing of your faith produces
patience. But let patience have its perfect work,
that you may be perfect and complete,
lacking nothing.

JAMES 1:2-4 NKJV

In this you greatly rejoice, though now for a
little while you may have had to suffer grief
in all kinds of trials. These have come so that
your faith—of greater worth than gold, which
perishes even though refined by fire—may be
proved genuine and may result in praise, glory
and honor when Jesus Christ is revealed.

1 PETER 1:6-7 NIV

Beloved, do not think it strange concerning the fiery trial which is to try you, as though some strange thing happened to you; but rejoice to the extent that you partake of Christ's sufferings, that when His glory is revealed, you may also be glad with exceeding joy.

1 PETER 4:12-13 NKJV

God has promised strength for the day, rest for the labor, light for the way, grace for the trials, help from above, unfailing sympathy, undying love.

— *Annie Johnson Flint* —

AN
UNDERSTANDING HEART

I have not stopped giving thanks for you,
remembering you in my prayers. I keep asking
that the God of our Lord Jesus Christ,
the glorious Father, may give you the
Spirit of wisdom and revelation,
so that you may know him better.

EPHESIANS 1:16-17 NIV

Perfume and incense bring joy to the heart,
and the pleasantness of one's friend springs
from his earnest counsel.

PROVERBS 27:9 NIV

Where your treasure is,
there your heart will be also.

MATTHEW 6:21 ESV

Be completely humble and gentle; be patient,
bearing with one another in love. Make every
effort to keep the unity of the Spirit
through the bond of peace.

EPHESIANS 4:2-3 NIV

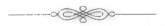

*There is much satisfaction in work
well done; praise is sweet, but there can
be no happiness equal to the joy
of finding a heart that understands.*

— *Victor Robinson* —

JOY BY FAITH

Now faith is the assurance of things hoped for, the conviction of things not seen. For by it the people of old received their commendation. By faith we understand that the universe was created by the word of God, so that what is seen was not made out of things that are visible.

HEBREWS 11:1-3 ESV

They that sow in tears shall reap in joy.

PSALM 126:5 KJV

Not that we lord it over your faith, but we work with you for your joy, because it is by faith you stand firm.

2 CORINTHIANS 1:24 NIV

Well done, good and faithful servant; you were faithful over a few things, I will make you ruler over many things. Enter into the joy of your lord.

MATTHEW 25:21 NKJV

If it can be verified, we don't need faith.... Faith is for that which lies on the other side of reason. Faith is what makes life bearable, with all its tragedies and ambiguities and sudden, startling joys.

— *Madeleine L'Engle* —

WALK WITH GOD

Take your everyday, ordinary life —
your sleeping, eating, going-to-work,
and walking-around life — and place it before
God as an offering. Embracing what God does
for you is the best thing you can do for him.

ROMANS 12:1 THE MESSAGE

For You, LORD, have made me glad
through Your work;
I will triumph in the works of Your hands.
O LORD, how great are Your works!
Your thoughts are very deep.

PSALM 92:4-5 NKJV

He has showed you, O man, what is good.
And what does the LORD require of you?
To act justly and to love mercy and to walk
humbly with your God.

MICAH 6:8 NIV

*Joy is more than my spontaneous
expression of laughter, gaiety, and lightness.
It is deeper than an emotional expression
of happiness. Joy is a growing,
evolving manifestation of God.*

— Bonnie Monson —

FULL OF JOY

Even though the fig trees have no blossoms,
and there are no grapes on the vine;
even though the olive crop fails, and the fields
lie empty and barren...yet I will rejoice
in the Lord! I will be joyful in the God
of my salvation. The Sovereign Lord is my strength!

HABAKKUK 3:17-19 NLT

Open your mouth and taste,
open your eyes and see—
how good GOD is.
Blessed are you who run to him.
Worship GOD if you want the best;
worship opens doors to all his goodness.

PSALM 34:8-9 THE MESSAGE

Their hearts may be encouraged, having been
knit together in love, and attaining to all
the wealth that comes from the full assurance
of understanding, resulting in a true knowledge
of God's mystery, that is, Christ Himself.

COLOSSIANS 2:2 NASB

*When I think upon my God,
my heart is so full of joy that the notes
dance and leap from my pen.*

— *Franz Josef Haydn* —

DREAM

Afterward,
I will pour out my Spirit on all people.
Your sons and daughters will prophesy,
your old men will dream dreams,
your young men will see visions.
Even on my servants, both men and women,
I will pour out my Spirit in those days.
I will show wonders in the heavens
and on the earth.

JOEL 2:28-30 NIV

In all my prayers for all of you,
I always pray with joy.

PHILIPPIANS 1:4 NIV

A dream fulfilled is a tree of life.

PROVERBS 13:12 NLT

I came so they can have
real and eternal life, more and better life
than they ever dreamed of.

JOHN 10:10 THE MESSAGE

*Always stay connected to people and seek
out things that bring you joy.
Dream with abandon. Pray confidently.*

— *Barbara Johnson* —

STEADFAST JOY

The steadfast love of the LORD never ceases;
his mercies never come to an end;
they are new every morning;
great is your faithfulness.

LAMENTATIONS 3:22-23 ESV

The sound of joyful shouting and salvation
is in the tents of the righteous;
The right hand of the LORD does valiantly.

PSALM 118:15 NASB

For the LORD is good and his love endures forever;
his faithfulness continues through all generations.

PSALM 100:5 NIV

I will exalt you, my God the King; I will praise your name for ever and ever. Every day I will praise you and extol your name for ever and ever. Great is the LORD and most worthy of praise; his greatness no one can fathom.

PSALM 145:1-3 NIV

[God] stands fast as your rock, steadfast as your safeguard, sleepless as your watcher, valiant as your champion.

— *Charles H. Spurgeon* —

NAME OF NAMES

Wherefore God also hath highly exalted him,
and given him a name which is above every name:
That at the name of Jesus every knee should
bow, of things in heaven, and things in earth,
and things under the earth; And that every
tongue should confess that Jesus Christ is Lord,
to the glory of God the Father.

PHILIPPIANS 2:9-11 KJV

From the rising of the sun to its setting,
the name of the LORD is to be praised!
The LORD is high above all nations,
and his glory above the heavens!

PSALM 113:3-4 ESV

For a child will be born to us,

a son will be given to us;

And the government will rest on His shoulders;

And His name will be called

Wonderful Counselor, Mighty God,

Eternal Father, Prince of Peace.

ISAIAH 9:6 NASB

*Even when I acknowledge You as
someone who has no need of me...
even then I have called You once again
by the same name, God of my life.*

— *Karl Rahner* —

KNOW GOD,
KNOW JOY

So let us know, let us press on to know the LORD....

He will come to us like the rain,

Like the spring rain watering the earth.

HOSEA 6:3 NASB

Know that the LORD is God.

It is he who made us, and we are his;

We are his people, the sheep of his pasture.

PSALM 100:3 NIV

For to the one who pleases him God has given

wisdom and knowledge and joy.

ECCLESIASTES 2:26 ESV

Then I will give them a heart to know Me,
that I am the LORD; and they shall be
My people, and I will be their God, for they
shall return to Me with their whole heart.

JEREMIAH 24:7 NKJV

*There is no joy comparable to the joy of
discovering something new from God,
about God. If the continuing life is a life
of joy, we will go on discovering, learning.*

— Eugenia Price —

JOY AND PRAISE

When I remember these *things*,
I pour out my soul within me.
For I used to go with the multitude;
I went with them to the house of God,
With the voice of joy and praise.

PSALM 42:4 NKJV

You shall rejoice before the LORD your God,
you and your sons and daughters.

DEUTERONOMY 12:11 NASB

The precepts of the LORD are right,
giving joy to the heart.
The commands of the LORD are radiant,
giving light to the eyes.

PSALM 19:8 NIV

It is my prayer that your love may abound more and more, with knowledge and all discernment, so that you may approve what is excellent, and so be pure and blameless for the day of Christ, filled with the fruit of righteousness that comes through Jesus Christ, to the glory and praise of God.

PHILIPPIANS 1:9-11 ESV

May your life become one of glad and unending praise to the Lord as you journey through this world!

— *Teresa of Avila* —

MY REFUGE

Love the Lord your God with all your heart
and with all your soul and with all your strength
and with all your mind.

LUKE 10:27 NIV

Hear my cry, O God;
Give heed to my prayer.
From the end of the earth I call to You
when my heart is faint;
Lead me to the rock that is higher than I.
For You have been a refuge for me,
A tower of strength against the enemy.
Let me dwell in Your tent forever;
Let me take refuge in the shelter of Your wings.

PSALM 61:1-4 NASB

God is our refuge and strength,

an ever-present help in trouble.

Therefore we will not fear,

though the earth give way

and the mountains fall into the heart of the sea,

though its waters roar and foam.

PSALM 46:1-3 NIV

When you accept the fact that sometimes seasons are dry and times are hard and that God is in control of both, you will discover a sense of divine refuge.

— *Charles R. Swindoll* —

JOY IN WORSHIP

Worship the LORD with reverence
And rejoice with trembling.

PSALM 2:11 NASB

I have trusted in Your lovingkindness;
My heart shall rejoice in Your salvation.
I will sing to the LORD,
Because He has dealt bountifully with me.

PSALM 13:5-6 NASB

All the earth worships you
and sings praises to you;
they sing praises to your name.

PSALM 66:4 ESV

The LORD is my strength and my song;
he has become my salvation.
He is my God, and I will praise him,
my father's God, and I will exalt him....
Who is like you—majestic in holiness,
awesome in glory, working wonders?

EXODUS 15:2, 11 NIV

Let us give all that lies within us...
to pure praise, to pure loving adoration,
and to worship from a grateful heart—
a heart that is trained to look up.

— Amy Carmichael —

RIGHTEOUS JOY

The prospect of the righteous is joy,
but the hopes of the wicked come to nothing.

PROVERBS 10:28 NIV

Fall on your knees and pray—to God's delight!
You'll see God's smile and celebrate,
finding yourself set right with God.
You'll sing God's praises to everyone you meet.

JOB 33:26-27 NLT

He who sows righteousness reaps a sure reward....
Those who are righteous will go free.

PROVERBS 11:18, 21 NIV

The mouth of the righteous is a fountain of life,
but the mouth of the wicked conceals violence.
Hatred stirs up strife,
but love covers all offenses.

PROVERBS 10:11-12 ESV

*We are forgiven and righteous because of
Christ's sacrifice; therefore we are pleasing
to God in spite of our failures.
Christ alone is the source of our
forgiveness, freedom, joy, and purpose.*

— *Robert S. McGee* —

MEETING NEEDS

His divine power has given us everything
we need for life and godliness through our
knowledge of him who called us by his own
glory and goodness.

2 PETER 1:3 NIV

My God shall supply all your need according
to his riches in glory in Christ Jesus. Now unto
God and our Father be glory for ever and ever.

PHILIPPIANS 4:19-20 KJV

I am the one who answers
your prayers and cares for you.
I am like a tree that is always green;
all your fruit comes from me.

HOSEA 14:8 NLT

Steep yourself in God-reality, God-initiative, God-provisions. You'll find all your everyday human concerns will be met. Don't be afraid of missing out. You're my dearest friends! The Father wants to give you the very kingdom itself.

LUKE 12:29-32 THE MESSAGE

If you have a special need today, focus your full attention on the goodness and greatness of your Father rather than on the size of your need. Your need is so small compared to His ability to meet it.

LORD BLESS YOU

The LORD bless you and keep you;
The LORD make His face shine upon you,
And be gracious to you;
The LORD lift up His countenance upon you,
And give you peace.

NUMBERS 6:24-26 NKJV

A faithful man will abound with blessings.

PROVERBS 28:20 ESV

May the favor of the Lord our God rest upon us;
establish the work of our hands for us—
yes, establish the work of our hands.

PSALM 90:17 NIV

Blessed be the God and Father of our
Lord Jesus Christ, who has blessed us
with every spiritual blessing.

EPHESIANS 1:3 NASB

*There are two requirements for our...
earthly blessing which God bestows
on us—a thankful reflection on the
goodness of the Giver and a deep sense of
the unworthiness of the receiver.
The first would make us grateful,
the second humble.*

— Hannah More —

107

A FRIEND'S LOVE

Let love and faithfulness never leave you;
bind them around your neck,
write them on the tablet of your heart.

PROVERBS 3:3 NIV

A new commandment I give to you, that you
love one another, even as I have loved you,
that you also love one another.

JOHN 13:34 NASB

Be imitators of God, therefore, as dearly loved
children and live a life of love, just as Christ
loved us and gave himself up for us as a fragrant
offering and sacrifice to God.

EPHESIANS 5:1-2 NIV

Love is patient and kind; love does not envy or boast; it is not arrogant or rude. It does not insist on its own way; it is not irritable or resentful; it does not rejoice at wrongdoing, but rejoices with the truth. Love bears all things, believes all things, hopes all things, endures all things. Love never ends.

1 CORINTHIANS 13:4-8 NKJV

What brings joy to the heart is not so much the friend's gifts as the friend's love.

— *Aelred of Rievaulx* —

109

THE GIFT OF JOY

God…made us alive together with Christ…
and raised us up with him and seated us with
him in the heavenly places in Christ Jesus,
so that in the coming ages he might show the
immeasurable riches of his grace in kindness
toward us in Christ Jesus. For by grace you
have been saved through faith. And this is not
your own doing; it is the gift of God, not a result
of works, so that no one may boast.

EPHESIANS 2:5-9 ESV

Our hearts ache, but we always have joy.
We are poor, but we give spiritual riches to others.
We own nothing, and yet we have everything.

2 CORINTHIANS 6:10 NLT

Every good and perfect gift is from above,
coming down from the Father of the heavenly
lights, who does not change like shifting shadows.

JAMES 1:17 NIV

Isn't everything you have and everything
you are sheer gifts from God?

1 CORINTHIANS 4:7 THE MESSAGE

*Stretch out your hand and take the
world's wide gift of Joy and Beauty.*

— *Corinne Roosevelt Robinson* —

STAND IN GRACE

But none of these things move me; nor do I count my life dear to myself, so that I may finish my race with joy, and the ministry which I received from the Lord Jesus, to testify to the gospel of the grace of God.

ACTS 20:24 NKJV

Therefore, since we have been justified through faith, we have peace with God through our Lord Jesus Christ, through whom we have gained access by faith into this grace in which we now stand. And we rejoice in the hope of the glory of God.

ROMANS 5:1-2 NIV

Whom have I in heaven but you?
And earth has nothing I desire besides you.
My flesh and my heart may fail,
but God is the strength of my heart
and my portion forever.

PSALM 73:25-26 NIV

*Among our treasures are such wonderful
things as the grace of Christ, the love of
Christ, the joy and peace of Christ.*

— L. B. Cowman —

SOMETHING BEAUTIFUL

Give to the LORD glory and strength.
Give to the LORD the glory due His name;
Bring an offering, and come before Him.
Oh, worship the LORD in the beauty of holiness!
Tremble before Him, all the earth.
The world also is firmly established,
It shall not be moved.

1 CHRONICLES 16:28-30 NKJV

Do not let your adorning be external —
the braiding of hair and the putting on of gold
jewelry, or the clothing you wear — but let your
adorning be the hidden person of the heart with
the imperishable beauty of a gentle and quiet
spirit, which in God's sight is very precious.

1 PETER 3:3-4 ESV

One thing I have asked from the LORD,
that I shall seek:
That I may dwell in the house of the LORD
all the days of my life,
To behold the beauty of the LORD
And to meditate in His temple.

PSALM 27:4 NASB

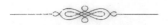

*We need to recapture the power of
imagination; we shall find that life can be
full of wonder, mystery, beauty, and joy.*

— *Sir Harold Spencer Jones* —

THE JOY OF REST

Come to me, all you who are weary and
burdened, and I will give you rest. Take my
yoke upon you and learn from me, for I am
gentle and humble in heart, and you
will find rest for your souls.

MATTHEW 11:28-29 NIV

Rest in the LORD, and wait patiently for him.

PSALM 37:7 KJV

He who dwells in the shelter of the Most High
Will abide in the shadow of the Almighty.
I will say to the LORD,
"My refuge and my fortress,
My God, in whom I trust!"

PSALM 91:1-2 NASB

The LORD is my shepherd, I shall not be in want.

He makes me lie down in green pastures,

he leads me beside quiet waters,

he restores my soul.

PSALM 23:1-3 NIV

Let the day suffice, with all its joys and failings, its little triumphs and defeats. I'd happily, if sleepily, welcome evening as a time of rest, and let it slip away, losing nothing.

— *Kathleen Norris* —

DELIGHT
IN PRAISE

Delight yourself in the LORD
and he will give you the desires of your heart.
Commit your way to the LORD;
trust in him and he will do this:
He will make your righteousness
shine like the dawn,
the justice of your cause like the noonday sun.

PSALM 37:4-6 NIV

I delight to do thy will, O my God.

PSALM 40:8 KJV

He will be a joy and delight to you, and many
will rejoice because of his birth.

LUKE 1:14 NIV

The LORD your God is with you,

he is mighty to save.

He will take great delight in you,

he will quiet you with his love,

he will rejoice over you with singing.

ZEPHANIAH 3:17 NIV

Like supernatural effervescence, praise will sometimes bubble up from the joy of simply knowing Christ. Praise like that is... delight. Pure pleasure! But praise can also be supernatural determination.

— Joni Eareckson Tada —

FROM GOD'S HAND

GOD your God, will cut away the thick calluses
on your heart and your children's hearts,
freeing you to love GOD, your God, with your
whole heart and soul and live, really live.
GOD, your God, will put all these curses on
your enemies who hated you and were out
to get you. And you will make a new start,
listening obediently to GOD, keeping all his
commandments that I'm commanding you
today. GOD, your God, will outdo himself
in making things go well for you: you'll...
enjoy an all-around good life. Yes, GOD
will start enjoying you again, making things
go well for you just as he enjoyed doing it
for your ancestors.

DEUTERONOMY 30:6-9 THE MESSAGE

Who among all these does not know
that the hand of the LORD has done this?
In his hand is the life of every living thing
and the breath of all mankind.

JOB 12:9-10 ESV

*Life itself, every bit of health that
we enjoy, every hour of...free enjoyment,
the ability to see, to hear, to speak,
to think, and to imagine—all this
comes from the hand of God.*

— Billy Graham —

HIS PRESENCE

We know that the one who raised the Lord
Jesus from the dead will also raise us with
Jesus and present us with you in his presence.
All this is for your benefit, so that the grace that
is reaching more and more people may cause
thanksgiving to overflow to the glory of God.

2 CORINTHIANS 4:14-15 NIV

Now to him who is able to keep you from
stumbling and to present you blameless before
the presence of his glory with great joy, to the
only God, our Savior, through Jesus Christ
our Lord, be glory, majesty, dominion, and
authority, before all time and now and forever.

JUDE 1:24-25 ESV

As for me, You uphold me in my integrity,

And You set me in Your presence forever.

Blessed be the LORD, the God of Israel,

From everlasting to everlasting.

PSALM 41:12-13 NASB

Jesus Christ has brought every need, every joy, every gratitude, every hope of men before God. He accompanies us and brings us into the presence of God.

— Dietrich Bonhoeffer —

GRACE

Grace and peace be yours in abundance through
the knowledge of God and of Jesus our Lord....
Through these he has given us his very great
and precious promises.

2 PETER 1:2, 4 NIV

Grace to you and peace from God our Father
and the Lord Jesus Christ. Blessed be the God
and Father of our Lord Jesus Christ, the Father
of mercies and God of all comfort, who comforts
us in all our affliction, so that we may be able to
comfort those who are in any affliction,
with the comfort with which we ourselves
are comforted by God.

2 CORINTHIANS 1:2-4 ESV

A joyful heart makes a cheerful face....
A cheerful heart has a continual feast.

PROVERBS 15:13, 15 NASB

Grace to you and peace from God our Father
and the Lord Jesus Christ.

ROMANS 1:7 NKJV

Grace creates liberated laughter.
The grace of God...is beautiful,
and it radiates joy and awakens humor.

— Karl Barth —

UNTAINTED HEART

Blessed are the pure in heart:
for they shall see God.

MATTHEW 5:8 KJV

Their life shall be like a watered garden,
and they shall languish no more.
Then shall the young women rejoice in the dance,
and the young men and the old shall be merry.
I will turn their mourning into joy.

JEREMIAH 31:12-13 ESV

Watch over your heart with all diligence,
For from it flow the springs of life.

PROVERBS 4:23 NASB

The LORD will guide you always;
he will satisfy your needs in a sun-scorched land
and will strengthen your frame.
You will be like a well-watered garden,
like a spring whose waters never fail.

ISAIAH 58:11 NIV

*At heart, the symbolism of the garden
relates back to Eden, where the wonder
and joy of God's creation was new and
fresh and untainted.*

— *Philip Glassborow* —

PASS IT ON

Let us keep the joy of loving Jesus in our hearts.
And let's share that joy with everyone we meet.
Passing on joy is something which is very
natural. We have no reason for not being joyful,
since Christ is with us. Christ is in our hearts.

MOTHER TERESA